The

BOOK

of

KELLE

BOOKS BY LOCHLAINN SEABROOK (alphabetized)

Abraham Lincoln: The Southern View - Demythologizing America's Sixteenth
      President
Aphrodite's Trade: The Hidden History of Prostitution Unveiled
A Rebel Born: A Defense of Nathan Bedford Forrest - Confederate General, American
      Legend
Britannia Rules: Goddess-Worship in Ancient Anglo-Celtic Society - An Academic
      Look at the United Kingdom's Matricentric Spiritual Past
Carnton Plantation Ghost Stories: True Tales of the Unexplained from Tennessee's
      Most Haunted Civil War House!
Christmas Before Christianity: How the Birthday of the "Sun" Became the Birthday of
      the "Son"
Nathan Bedford Forrest: Southern Hero, American Patriot - Honoring a Confederate
      Icon and the Old South
Princess Diana: Modern-Day Moon-Goddess - A Psychoanalytical and Mythological
      Look at Diana Spencer's Life, Marriage, and Death
The Blakeneys: An Etymological and Ethnological Study - Unveiling the Mysterious
      Origins of the Blakeney Family and Name
The Book of Kelle: An Introduction to Goddess-Worship and the Great Celtic Mother-
      Goddess Kelle, Original Blessed Lady of Ireland
The Caudills: An Etymological, Ethnological, and Genealogical Study - Exploring the
      Name and National Origins of a European-American Family
The Goddess Dictionary of Words and Phrases: Introducing a New Core Vocabulary for
      the Women's Spirituality Movement
The McGavocks of Carnton Plantation: A Southern History - Celebrating One of
      Dixie's Most Noble Confederate Families and Their Tennessee Home
UFOs and Aliens: The Complete Guidebook

To order or for more information, please visit the publisher's Website:
www.searavenpress.com

SEA RAVEN PRESS

Thought Provoking Books For Smart People

The Book of

KELLE

An Introduction to Goddess-Worship
Of the Great Celtic Mother Goddess Kelle
Original Blessed Lady of Ireland

Lochlainn Seabrook

SEA RAVEN PRESS

THE BOOK OF KELLE

Second edition, second printing

Published by Sea Raven Press
P.O. Box 1054, Franklin, Tennessee 37065-1054
www.searavenpress.com • searavenpress@nii.net
Thought Provoking Books For Smart People

First edition, first printing - June 1999
Second edition, first printing - June 2010
Second edition, second printing - July 2010

ISBN: 978-0-9827700-1-6

Library of Congress Catalog Number: 2010929131

The Book of Kelle: An Introduction to Goddess-Worship and the Great Celtic
Mother-Goddess Kelle, Original Blessed Lady of Ireland/Lochlainn Seabrook.
Includes biographical references and index.

Front and back cover design, book design and layout, by Lochlainn Seabrook
Front cover photo, Goddess triple spiral pendant, by Lochlainn Seabrook
Typography: Sea Raven Press

Printed and manufactured in occupied Tennessee, former Confederate States of America

 Dedication

Dedicated to Kelle and to her mortal descendants,
the author's ancestors, the Kelly family.

 Epigraph

The Lord hath created a new thing in the earth:
a woman shall compass a man.

Jeremiah 31:22

Contents

The Goddess-worshiping Celts

Introduction

It has long been held by most theologians, anthropologists, and other academicians that the world has never known pure Goddess-worship. In particular they deny that it ever existed in the British Isles. Actually, the exact reverse is true.

For the vast majority of the islands' history the veneration of a female Supreme Being (Mother-Goddess) was the only religion known. Indeed, until the Early Neolithic Age, about 4,500 BCE, the concept of a male deity (Father-God) did not even exist in Europe.

As I will show, proof of Anglo-Celtic Goddess-worship is overwhelming and plentiful. The nations of Britain, Ireland, and Scotland themselves, for example, were all named after goddesses, as were many of their rivers, islands, towns, hills, and mountains.

Reinforcing this evidence is the fact that many surrounding countries and regions also take their names from female deities. Among these we have Italy, Holland, Denmark, Crete, Malta, Albania, and Scandinavia, just to name a few. Europe herself is named after a goddess, as is our planet, and even our universe.

While I will touch on these various topics, the final focus of this book is on the Goddess Kelle, who gave her name to her most ardent followers: the Kelts or Celts. Known by poets as "the Blessed Lady of Ireland," Kelle's story is a rich and fascinating one; one that I will trace back to early Asia, where she is still worshiped to this day as the Goddess Kali.

We will begin our quest to discover the Goddess Kelle with an introduction to thealogy: female based matricentric religion.

LOCHLAINN SEABROOK ⊗
Franklin, Tennessee, USA
June 1, 2010[1]

---

[1] June 1 is the Holy Day of the Roman Goddess Juno, after whom this month is named. Juno is known to the Greeks as Hera, to Jews as Asherah, to Christians as Mary, and to the Celts as Kelle.

The

Book

of

KELLE

1

The Evolution of Goddess-Worship

THOUGH THOUSANDS OF female deities have been, and continue to be, embraced by the world's nearly infinite number of religions, all ultimately derive from a single spiritual and archetypal source: Goddess, variously known as the Great Mother, the Virgin, Mother-Earth, or the Moon-Goddess, the kindly, peaceful maternal figure who tenderly watches over her earthly offspring.[2]

Long before the emergence of the idea of a male "God," this feminine deity, whom we shall refer to simply as "Goddess," was worshiped as the "Creatress of the Universe and all life." This makes her, of course, the original Supreme Being and the forerunner of all male deities.

Why was a female Supreme Being venerated before a male one? The answer is elementary: it is the female who creates life within her body.

---

[2] Later, Goddess was portrayed more realistically, with all of the complexities and different aspects of femaleness that ordinary human women possess. This more believable depiction revealed not only the Great Mother's loving side, but her violent side as well, giving rise to such "dark" goddesses as the ancient Egyptian Sekhmet, the Aztec Coatlicue, the Greek Enyo, the Celtic Cailleach, and the Hindu Kali. Note: Cailleach is a variation of the Celtic Goddess Kelle, the subject of this book, while Kelle herself is a variation of the much older Kali.

In prehistoric times people were not aware of the male contribution to the process of reproduction. In this prescientific period they could not have possibly known of the connection between copulation and fertilization. Thus the male's role in insemination was completely unperceived.

Because of this, women were long considered not only superior to men, but more importantly they were believed to be parthenogenic (from the Greek *parthenos*, meaning "virgin," and the Latin *genesis*, meaning "birth"); [3] that is, they were seen as virgin-mothers who created life independently and magically within their own bodies.

This imbued the female with incredible sacrality,

---

[3] The Latin word *genesis* derives from the Greek word *gignesthai*, meaning "to be born." From here we also get the words gene and genetics.

numenistic power, and spiritual force, while essentially relegating the male to the position of subordinate. To this day there are still living archaic peoples who are not aware of the role of the male in reproduction, so we should not be surprised to learn that humans living hundreds of thousands of years ago were also ignorant of this fact.

From this we would expect prehistoric peoples to venerate the Supreme Being in the form of, not a male Father-God, but a Mother-Goddess; or more precisely, a Virgin-Mother-Goddess. And this is exactly what occurred.

As early as 500,000 years ago (during the Acheulian Period of the Lower Paleolithic Age), *Homo erectus* was carving crude female figurines in her honor, while between 100,000 and 40,000 years ago the Neanderthal people were burying their dead with roughly made triangular-shaped stones (the three-sided shape represents Goddess' life-giving pubic triangle), flowers (a decidedly feminine symbol), and red ochre (red being the color of the female's life-bearing menstrual blood).

Some 15,000 years ago, the religion of the Great Goddess manifested artistically in beautifully designed figurines of faceless, large-breasted women, with shelf-like buttocks and swollen (pregnant) abdomens. These are the so-called (and misnamed) "Venuses" of the Cro-Magnon people.[4]

---

[4] They are misnamed because these particular Goddess figurines had nothing to do with sex (Venus is the Roman Sex-Goddess). Rather they were carved as sacred images of the Divine Feminine or Female Principle, and of Woman's bounteous life-giving power as embodied in the Great Virgin-Mother-Goddess. Despite this obvious fact, some anthropologists (mainly male ones) have postulated that the Venus statuettes were used by prehistoric peoples as "pornographic images," a preposterous theory by any standard.

So powerful and enduring was the religion of Goddess in ages past that not a single image of a male deity appears in the fossil record until a mere 6,000 years ago. Why do masculine representations of gods begin to only show up at this late period specifically?

In Europe, at least, matricentric, matrifocal, matrilineal culture, religion, and society reached its zenith among the amazing Minoans of ancient Crete, where egalitarianism, happiness, and prosperity reigned from about 5,000 to 3,375 years ago. It was around the latter date, 1,375 BCE, that what is known as the Patriarchal Takeover hit Crete with full force, culminating in the destruction of her political and religious capitol, the city of Knossos.

The Patriarchal Takeover had swept over other parts of

Europe much sooner, as early as around 4,000 BCE, completely transforming entire regions from female-dominant to male-dominant societies.

For those who doubt its reality, it was well chronicled in early mythology, such as in the Greek legend of Hercules (Heracles), who steals the magic girdle (waist belt) of the Amazonian Queen Hippolyta (thereby disempowering her, and, by extension, all women).

The Patriarchal Takeover is even documented in the Bible, one example being that of the ancient Hebrew story of the Goddess-worshiping Judean Queen Athaliah, who was ruthlessly executed by God-worshiping priests for her beliefs (see 2 Kings 10:1-36; 11:1-16).[5]

---

[5] Other early Jewish women who tried to retain or revive Goddess-worship met a similar fate, such as Jezebel, who was brutally murdered for following the female-based religion of her ancestors (see 1 Kings 16:31-33; 2 Kings 9:22, 30-37). Another, Queen

The world-altering Takeover began when aggressive, horse-back riding, patricentric tribes charged out of southwestern Russia (near the Black Sea), and overran the peaceful agrarian communities of Goddess-worshipers—known collectively and globally as the Matriarchate—that were then spread out over the whole of Europe and Asia.

This momentous event, the overthrow of the Matriarchate and the establishment of the Patriarchate, was triggered, in great part, by a simple discovery: by 6,000 BCE the knowledge of the domestication of wild animals had been acquired through intentional selective breeding. From that point on, people were no longer bound to the soil and farming. If a drought came and

---

Maacha of Judea, was dethroned for worshiping Goddess (in the shape of an idol of the Goddess Asherah) in a sacred tree grove (1 Kings 15:9-13).

crops failed, or if wanderlust struck, the new herdsmen could now simply pick up and travel to a new location, bringing their primary food source with them, for domesticated livestock, unlike vegetable farms, were portable.

A natural outcome of the discovery of animal domestication was that the male's role in reproduction was finally revealed. With the Masculine Principle (fatherhood) now uncovered, men inevitably rebelled against their subordinate roles and inferior social status.

In Europe (and other portions of the globe) the result was the Patriarchal Takeover, with all of its attendant turbulence and trauma, for the peaceful farmers of the prehistoric matricentric world were no match for the newly arriving antagonistic, violent breeders and herders.

In opposition to the life-giving Earth-Virgin-Mother-Goddess of the Matriarchate, whose celestial symbol was the Moon, the new all-male Patriarchate set up a masculine-based religion whose followers now saw the Divine as made in their own image.

Thus there emerged for the first time in human evolution the idea of a *male* Supreme Being, a deity envisioned by prehistoric men as a stern and aggressive Sky-Father-God, who ruled the world using psychological intimidation (for example, the threat of eternal damnation) and physical force (symbolized by the lightning bolt and the smithy's hammer). His celestial symbol, of course, was the Sun.

The new God ordered the overthrow of the Matriarchate, the suppression of Goddess-worship, and the destruction of Goddess' Temples, a process that was still under way 4,500 years later, well into the 1st Century CE, as the New Testament notes (see, for instance, Acts 19:27).

The twenty-eight-day-month, thirteen-month Lunar Calender of the Goddess-worshipers was suppressed, replaced by the thirty-day-month, twelve-month Solar Calender of the God-worshipers. Moon-Day (Monday), the sacred day of the Matriarchate, was tossed out, supplanted by the new sacred day of the Patriarchate: Sun-Day (Sunday).

The Mother-Goddess was knocked off her throne as the Supreme Being, exchanged for the new Father-God, the Divine Sun—or Divine Son, as he would come to be popularly known.

In the process of ousting the Earth-Mother for the Sky-Father, female spirituality (essentially Pagan mysticism) and the feminine concern for the Earth (farming and ecology) were superseded by male spirituality (essentially orthodox religion) and the masculine concern for intellectual matters (industry and philosophy).

About this time, weapons (that is, implements for killing humans) begin to appear in the fossil record for the first time. Many other such dramatic changes occurred too numerous to mention in a mere introduction on this topic.[6]

The imposition of a masculine spiritual belief system on the world did not bring Goddess-worship to a complete

---

[6] For a more detailed treatment of the Matriarchate and the Patriarchal Takeover, see the Introduction in my book, *The Goddess Dictionary of Words and Phrases.*

halt, as might be supposed. Instead, now demoted, Goddess began to share her throne with the new God as his consort or wife.

Well-known examples of this occurred in ancient Egypt with the Father-God Osiris and the Mother-Goddess Isis; in ancient Greece with the Father-God Zeus and the Mother-Goddess Hera; in ancient Israel with the Father-God Yahweh and the Mother-Goddess Asherah; and in ancient Rome with the Father-God Jupiter and the Mother-Goddess Juno.

In time, however, most male-based religions submerged Goddess altogether (this occurred most notably in the orthodox or male—as opposed to the mystical or feminine—branches of Judaism, Christianity, and Islam), transforming her into various saints, "holy spirits," angels, or demons, or more often, subsuming her into the "virgin-mother" of the new male Supreme Being.

Examples of this new type of relationship include the Virgin-Mother Persephone and her Savior-Son Dionysus; the Virgin-Mother Alcmene and her Savior-Son Heracles; the Virgin-Mother Juno and her Savior-Son Mars; and, of course, the Virgin-Mother Mary and her Savior-Son Jesus (known in Greek mythology as Jason).

Thus, though in her role as the sole Supreme Being she has been expelled by mainstream Western religions, to this day Goddess is still venerated, in one form or another, by nearly all of the world's faiths, even the most patriarchal.

For instance, among mystical (Gnostic) Christians she is

still worshiped as Sophia Mari; to mainstream Christians she is the Virgin Mary; among mystical Jews she is Asherah, Zion, or Shekinah; and among mystical Muslims she is the Arabian "Queen of Heaven," Allat.

To Buddhists she is called Mara; to the Greeks she is Maia; to the Egyptians she is known as Isis or Meri; in the Middle East she is Ishtar; and across Europe she is still called t!.e May Queen, or Maid Marian.

We will note here that the *ma*, *mar*, and *mari* elements found in many of Goddess' names comes from the connection between the Female Principle (that is, mother or mama) and water, and more specifically sea water. Why?

The ancients believed the ocean to be Goddess' salty

amniotic fluid, the worldwide body of water out of which all life was formed and born (mirrored in the pregnant human female, an earthly version of the Great Virgin-Mother-Goddess).

The linguistic link that connects Goddess, human females, water, and the *ma / mar* names derives from the Latin word *mare* for ocean (marine), the plural of which is *maria*. Thus the Virgin Mary still goes by one of the titles of the great pre-Christian, Pagan Virgin-Mother-Goddess: Stella Maris ("Star of the Sea").

It is from these ancient words that we get the following women's names, many of them various names of Goddess: Mara, Mare, Maren, Maret, Margaret, Margaux, Margery, Marghanita, Margot, Margrita, Mari, Maria, Mariah, Mariam, Mariamne, Marian, Mariana,

Marianella, Marie, Mariel, Mariene, Marily, Marilyn, Marin, Marina, Marion, Maris, Marisa, Mariska, Marjorie, Marla, Marlana, Marlene, Marley, Marlis, Marlo, Marna, Marrie, Marrim, Marsha, Marta, Martha, Marti, Martina, Martta, Mary, and Marya.

2

A Worldwide Pantheon of Goddesses

 S THE MILLENNIA have passed, the Great Mother, or The One, as she is also called, has been personified in a myriad of different guises by every known people, society, culture, religion, and nation.

The result has been a worldwide Pantheon of tens of thousands of goddesses, familiar to us today by a variety of local and regional names.

Some of the better known would include the following from this extremely abbreviated list (in alphabetical order):

ABUNDITA: the Roman Agriculture-Goddess who gave us the word abundance.

ACANTHA: the Greek Nymph-Goddess who gave us the name of the acanthus flower.

AETNA: the Roman Mountain-Goddess who gave her name to the Italian volcano, Mount Aetna.

ALBION: the Anglo-Celtic Moon-Goddess who gave England her earliest known name: Albion. Germany's Elbe River, the French city of Albi, the Italian city of Alba, and the country of Albania (also one of Scotland's ancient Roman names), were also named after her. Albion means "White Goddess," from the Latin *albus*, "white," which gives us such words as albino and albumen.

AMAZON: not a goddess, but an ancient, all-female nation of Goddess-worshiping warrior women, who gave their name to South America's most famous body of water, the Amazon, the largest river in the world. In ancient times fearsome Amazon tribes, some from an independent kingdom in Pontus (modern Turkey), roamed from Europe to Northern Africa, killing men, or maiming and enslaving them, to be used later for reproductive purposes. Male infants from these unions were instantly put to death, while daughters were lovingly nurtured into adulthood. Many modern anthropologists dismiss the Amazon as a figment of ancient imagination. But to do this they must ignore the written and spoken testimonies of early eyewitnesses, the numerous celebrated ancient historians who wrote in detail of them, countless ancient artistic images of Amazons (so plentiful are such artifacts that an entire genre of art was given the name amazonomachy, "Amazon battle"), and the nearly 3 million square-mile region that was named after them: Amazonia, or the Amazon Basin, as it is also known.

APHRODITE: one of the world's most important and influential female deities, this Greek Love-Goddess, whose name means born "out of [sea] foam," gives us the word aphrodisiac. Known elsewhere as Aphri or Afra, she also gave her name to both the continent of Africa and the month of April (from the Greek *Aphrilis*, "the sacred Moon phase of Aphrodite"). Additionally, her name was bestowed on the ancient Turkish city of Aphrodisias (or Aphroditius) as well as to one-half of the name of the Cyprian male-female deity Hermaphroditus, which in turn gives us the word hermaphrodite. Aphrodite in her trinitarian form was a triple-goddess known as Triple Aphrodite, mirrored in the Moirai, or the Three Fates, of Greek mythology: Klotho, Atropos, and Lachesis. Triple Aphrodite's sacred number was three,[7] which when triplicated (333) then doubled (that is, empowered), is 666. When her worship was suppressed by the early Catholic Church, her sacred number was demonized, becoming the dreaded number of "the Beast" (that is, Satan) with two backs, an allusion

---

[7] Like nearly all of the major goddesses, Aphrodite was linked to the number three because she ruled 1) birth, 2) life, and 3) death; or in some cases, 1) life, 2) death, and 3) rebirth. Thus the feminine number three possesses extreme sacrality and magicality, making Goddess the first Trinity, predating the emergence of the better known male Trinity by many thousands of years. Goddess' association with the number three is prehistoric, long exemplified in the beautiful triple spiral—like the one pictured on the cover of this book. For more on Aphrodite, and also on her connection to prostitution, see my book *Aphrodite's Trade: The Hidden History of Prostitution Unveiled.*

to Hermaphroditus, the Pagan Androgyne symbolizing sexual union (Revelation 13:18). But not even the orthodox Church's ban could hide the positive, powerful, sacred feminine beauty of the number 666, which is why the Christian creators of the Maze at Chartres Cathedral intentionally designed it to be precisely 666 feet in length. The Goddess-worshiping branch of the ancient Jews also understood and embraced the number. Hence, King Solomon (his name means the "Sun-God of On") received 666 "talents of gold" for his loyalty to the Israelite Matriarchate (1 Kings 10:14), governed by the famous Queen of Sheba (that is, the female head of the land of Arabia). As Sheba means "seven," Solomon's queen was just another personification of the Great Virgin-Mother-Goddess in her lunar form, whose sacred number seven multiplied by four equals twenty-eight, the numbers of days in a lunar month and the number of days of the female menstrual cycle.

ARACHNE: the Greek Weaver-Goddess after whom the class of arthropods known as the *Arachnida* (spiders, mites, scorpions, and ticks) is named. Her name means "spider."

ARARAT: the Anatolian Creatress-Goddess who gave her name to Mount Ararat (in modern day Armenia), made famous in the Hebrew legend of the Great Flood (Genesis 8:4), a tale that was in turn borrowed from the earlier Pagan Babylonians and Sumerians.

ARDUINNA: a Celtic Wilderness-Goddess who gave her name to the forests of Ardennes, Belgium.

ATHENE: also known as Athena, the sagacious Greek Mother-Goddess after whom the city of Athens, Greece, was named.

AURA: the Greek Mania-Goddess who gave us the word aura.

BASHO: the Japanese Goddess who gave her name to the basho plant.

BASILE: the title of many ancient Goddesses, from which we derive the word basilica (a type of early Christian church building). The word is Greek for "queen."

BERUTH: the Phoenician Mother-Earth-Goddess who gave her name to the city of Beirut, Lebanon. Her name literally means "Earth-Mother."

BIBLYS: the Greek Goddess who gave her name to the Christian Bible and to the ancient Phoenician city of Byblos (now known as Jubail, located on the coast of Lebanon), one of the oldest continually inhabited cities in the world.

BRIGID, BRIGANTIA, or BRIDE: the Anglo-Celtic Warrior-Goddess after whom Brittany, Britain, and the British people (the Britons) were named, as well as the Hebrides (He-Brides) Islands. To the Romans she was called Britannia, the poetic name that Britain is still known by.[8]

CARNA: the Roman Goddess who gave us the words carnation, carnivorous, carnage, carnival, carnivore,

---

[8] For an in-depth exploration of the Goddess Britannia, see my book, *Britannia Rules: Goddess-Worship in Ancient Anglo-Celtic Society*.

carnal, carnitine, corn, kernel, core, and cardiac.

CERES: the Latin Earth-Goddess from whom we get the word cereal.

CHI: the ancient Asian Life-Force-Goddess after whom the nation of China and the Chinese people were named.

COCOMAMA: the Andean Health-Goddess who gave her name to the coco plant. Her name means "Coco-Mother."

CONCORDIA: the Roman Peace-Goddess who gave us the word concord, meaning "harmony." Many American cities are named after this Goddess, such as Concord, North Carolina; Concord, New Hampshire; Concord, Massachusetts; and Concord, California.

COPIA: the Roman Abundance-Goddess who gave us the words copious and cornucopia.

CRETE: the Greek Goddess after whom the island of Crete was named.

CUBA: the Roman (Latin) Infant-Goddess after whom the West Indian island of Cuba was named (see next entry).

CYBELE: in ancient Rome, the Phrygian Mother-Goddess who gave her name to the black stone shrine in Mecca, Saudi Arabia, known today as the Kaaba, Kaabe, Ka'abe or Kubaba ("cube"). Scientists have discovered that a number of early goddesses were worshiped as cube-shaped stones, the earliest known reference being to one from Neolithic Anatolia (modern day Turkey).

Besides Cybele, other such goddesses include Astarte, Diana, Aphrodite, and Artemis. Cybele's cube-shaped stone was venerated in Rome at the beginning of the 2nd Century BCE. While today Cybele's name is said to mean "the Most Holy One," it was probably first spelled Cubaba or Kubaba, from *kuba* meaning "cube."

CYNOSURA: the Cretan Goddess who gave us the word cynosure (to "guide," or to be the "center of attention"), a word also applied to both the North Star and the constellation *Ursa Minor* (the Little Dipper), known in Greece as *Kynosoura*, from *kynos oura*: "dog's tail."

DA: the very ancient Greek Earth-Mother Goddess who gave us the name of the God Poseidon, whose name means "husband of Da."

DANA: the European Mother-Goddess who gave her name to Denmark and the Danish people, as well as to many European rivers (for example, the Danube, the Don, the Dnieper, and the Dniestr, among others). Celtic people everywhere claim descent from Dana, as their ancient name shows: *Tuatha de Danaan*, means "the People of Dana."

DEVI: the Hindu Mother-Goddess from whom we get the word divine. After Paganism was suppressed by the early Catholic Church, Devi's name was demonized and used as the basis for the name of the Christian evil-spirit-god, the "Devil."

DISCIPLINA: the Roman Goddess who gave us the word discipline.

DISCORDIA: the Roman Goddess of Chaos from whom we derive the word discord.

ECHIDNA: the Greek Goddess who gave her name to the animal of the same name, also known as the spiny anteater (of Australia, Tasmania, and New Guinea).

ECHO: the Greek Mountain-Goddess who gave us the modern English word echo.

EDDA: the "Eve" of the Norse Creation Legend, she gave her name, meaning "great-grandmother," to the Scandinavian holy books known as the *Eddas*: "Stories of [the] Great-Grandmother."

ELECTRA: the Greek Heroine-Goddess who gave us the words electric and electricity.

EOSTRE: the Anglo-Saxon Spring-Goddess who gave us the words Easter and estrus. Eostre's sacred animal (the fecund rabbit), her sacred fertility symbol (the egg), and her sacred color (green), all passed over into the celebration of Easter when the Pagan Holy Day was stolen and christianized by the Catholic Church. The Pagan method of calculating this sacred day using the lunar phases of the Moon-Goddess was also adopted by the Church and is still used to this day.

EPONA: the Saxon-Celtic Horse-Goddess who gave us the word pony.

ERDA: the ancient European Mother-Earth Goddess who gave her name to our planet, Earth.

ERIU: the Celtic Earth-Goddess who gave her name to

Ireland (meaning "Eriu's Land"), as well as to the Irish people.

EUROPA: the Cretan Moon-Mother-Goddess after whom the continent of Europe was named. Her name means "Broad-face" or "Wide-eyed," allusions to the Full Moon.

FAMA: the Roman Fame-Goddess (in Greece known as Pheme) who gave us the words fame and famous.

FLORA: the Roman Spring-Goddess who gave us the words floral, flowers, and flourish. Her name means "the Flourishing One."

FORTUNA: the Roman Good-Luck-Goddess who gave us the word fortune.

FRAUD: the Roman Treachery-Goddess who gave us the word fraud.

FRIGGA: the Sex-Goddess of northern Europe after whom our weekday Friday ("Frigga's Day") was named, and who also gave us the expletive frigging (meaning to masturbate or copulate).

FUJI: the Japanese Mountain-Goddess who gave her name to Mount Fuji, Japan's tallest natural elevation.

FULLA: the Scandinavian Abundance-Goddess who gave us the word full.

FURIES: the Greek Goddesses who gave us the word fury.

GALATEA: the Greek Milk-Goddess from whom we derive the word galaxy (meaning "Mother's Milk"), and who gave her name to the Gauls or Gaels (that is, the Celts) and their vast territory Galatia ("land of the Goddess Galatea"), as well as to the island of Malta (formerly known as Ma-Lat: "Mother Lat"). In her Italian form as the Goddess Latia, she gave her name to the Latin people: the Latins (the "followers of Latia"). She also gave us the word gala, a festive celebration, and the words lacto and lactic ("milk").

GANGA: the Hindu River-Goddess whom the sacred Ganges River in India is named after.

GODA: the ancient Hindu Mother-Goddess after whom the later emerging Father-Deity known as "God" was named. She also gave her name, of course, to the word

Goddess.

HALCYONE: the Greek Kingfisher-Goddess who gave us the word halcyon, meaning "happy" and "prosperous."

HARMONIA: the Greek Goddess who gave us the word harmony.

HEGEMONE: the Greek Goddess who gave us the word hegemony ("sovereignty").

HEL or HOL: the Teutonic Underworld-Goddess who gave her name to Holland (Hol's Land) and to the Christian underworld, Hell. Her name means "One Who Hides."

HERA: the ancient Greek Queen-Mother-Goddess who

gave us the name of the Greek Dying-and-Rising Savior-God Heracles ("Glory of Hera"), who was known in Rome as Hercules, and many of whose attributes were later artificially appended to the figure of Jesus by the early Catholic Church.[9] Hera means "Our Lady," a title later appropriated by Christians for their own Queen-Mother-Goddess, the mother of the Christian Heracles, the Virgin Mary.

HERO: the Greek Goddess who gave us the word hero.

IAHU: an ancient Hebrew Goddess and the oldest deity in Israel, she was later masculinized, giving her name to the later emerging patriarchal Father-God Yahweh (also

---

[9] Heracles was only one of dozens of Pagan deities whose attributes were, unfortunately, concretized onto Jesus. For more on the tragic subject of the paganization of Jesus, see my book, *Christmas Before Christianity: How the Birthday of the "Sun" Became the Birthday of the "Son."*

known variously as Jupiter, Jove, Jehovah, Jason, Jesus, and Zeus).

IDA: the Roman Goddess who gave her name to Mount Ida in Italy.

IRIS: the Greek Rainbow-Goddess who gave her name to the colored part of the eye, the iris. Her name means "rainbow."

ISIS: the ancient Egyptian Virgin-Mother-Goddess who (along with two male deities) gave her name to Israel (Isis-Ra-El) and its people, the Israelites, and who also served as one of the many prototypes for Christianity's Virgin-Mother-Goddess, Mary. With the absorption of Paganism by the Catholic Church (1st Century to 6th Century CE), pre-Christian images of Isis nursing her

Divine Son Horus later naturally passed into Christian mythology.

JUNO: the Roman Mother-Goddess of marriage and family life, after whom our month of June is named (as in ancient times, Juno's sacred month is still the favored time to wed).

KLOTHO: the Greek Fate-Goddess who spins the thread of life, and who gave us the word cloth.

KUNTI: the Indian Virgin-Mother-Goddess who gave her name to the all-sacred female pudenda.

LAMPETIA: the Greek Sun-Goddess who gave us the word lamp.

LIBERALITAS: the Roman Munificence-Goddess who gave us the words liberal and liberate.

LIBERTAS: the Roman Liberty-Goddess who gave us the word liberty.

LILITH: the Near-Eastern Mother-Goddess and original wife of Adam (and Judaism's first feminist), who gave us the word lily.

LOTIS: the Greek Nymph-Goddess who gave her name to the lotus tree and lotus flower.

LUATHS LURGANN: the Irish Midwife-Goddess who gave her name to Ireland's Loch Lurgann. Her name means "speedy foot."

LUNA: the Latin Moon-Goddess from whom we derive the words lunar and looney, and after whom our weekday Monday ("Moon's Day") is named (in Spanish Monday is *Lunes*; in French it is called *Lundi*; that is, "Luna's Day").

MABB: the Welsh Warrior-Goddess who appears in Shakespeare's play, *Romeo and Juliet*, as "Queen Mab."

MAGOG: the English Mountain-Goddess who gave her name to both the Gogmagog Hills and to Magg's Hills.

MAIA: the Roman Spring-Goddess who gave her name to the month of May. Her name means "Wise One."

MANIA: the Roman Frenzy-Goddess who gave us the word mania.

MANTO: the Greek Prophetess-Goddess who gave us the word mantic, meaning "prophetic powers."

MARA: the Germanic Witch-Goddess who gave us the word nightmare.

MARI: the Near-Eastern Virgin-Mother-Goddess from whom we get the word marriage (meaning "union under the auspices of the Goddess Mari"), who gave her name to the great Sumerian city of Mari (now known as *Tell Hariri* in modern day Syria), and who was later transformed into the Virgin "Mary" by Christian mythographers. The *ma* ("mother") and *mar* ("sea") elements of her name, as we have seen, are found in the names of numerous goddesses around the world, both ancient and modern, giving us the word marine: "Mother-Ocean."

MENS: the Roman Goddess who gave us the word menstruation. Her name derives from the same root as Moon: the Latin word *mensis* and the Greek word *men*, both meaning "month." The Greek word for Moon is *mene*.

METER: the Greek Mother-Goddess who gave us the words meter and matter. Her name means "mother."

MINTHE: the Roman Flower-Goddess who gave her name to the mint plant.

MONETA: the Roman Goddess of coinage who gave us the word money.

MORGAN LE FAY: the Celtic Death-Goddess whose sacred region Glamorgan (in Wales) gives us the word glamour, an early word for a witch's spell.

MORMO: the Greek female evil spirit from whom the Mormons (LDS, or the Church of Jesus Christ of Latter-Day Saints) took their name. The word Mormon literally means "Death-Moon" (from *mor*, "death," and *mon*, "Moon"). The name Mormo/Mormon refers to none other than the "Moon of Death," an allusion to Goddess in her "Mother of Destruction" form, identical to the Hindu Destroyer-of-Life-Goddess Kali-Ma, whose name means "Dark Mother." The name Mormo/Mormon is quite appropriate for one of the few Western faiths that still embraces a belief in the supreme Mother-Goddess. Mormo, said to bite disobedient children with her vampire-like fangs, was the companion of Hecate, another Greek version of the archetypal Moon-Goddess, known in Medieval times as the "Queen of the Witches."

MOROS: the terrifying Greek Night-Goddess from who we get the word morose.

MUSES, THE: the nine Greek Goddesses of art and inspiration who gave us the words muse and museum.

MYRRHA: the Near-Eastern Springtime-Goddess who gave us the name of the myrrh tree, mentioned in the canonical story of Jesus (Matthew 2:11).

NANA: the Scandinavian and Babylonian Crone-Goddess who gave us the nickname for grandmother: Nana. Her name means "Queen."

NECESSITAS: the Roman Fate-Goddess who gave us the words necessity and necessary.

NEMESIS: the Greek Revenge-Goddess who gave us the word nemesis, "enemy."

NIKE: the Greek Victory-Goddess who gave her name to the sportswear company of the same name. Her name means "victory."

NIX: the Germanic Water Sprite-Goddess (plural, Nixies) who gave us the word nix, meaning to "reject," "disagree," or "veto." She also gave her name to the spurious Christian figure Saint Nicholas or Saint Nick, later known in the West as Santa Claus.[10]

NYMPHEUOMENE: a title of the Greek Mother-Goddess Hera, which gave us the words nymphomania

---

[10] For a detailed discussion of this topic see my book, *Christmas Before Christianity: How the Birthday of the "Sun" Became the Birthday of the "Son."*

and nymphomaniac. The title means "She Who Takes a Mate."

OPS: the Roman Harvest-Goddess who gave us the word opulent.

PALES: the Roman Cattle-Goddess who gave her name to Palestine and her people, the Palestinians.

PORNE: "Harlot," one of the many titles of the Greek Sex-Goddess Aphrodite, and which gave us the word pornography, meaning the "writing of harlots."

PSYCHE: the Greek Soul-Goddess who gave her name to the modern science of psychology, literally meaning the "study of the soul."

ROMA: the Italian Love-Goddess who gave her name to the Roman Empire, to its people the Romans, to their capital city Rome, and also to the word romance (occultically, her name spelled backwards, *amor*, is the Latin word for "love").

SATI: the ancient Egyptian Serpent-Goddess after whom the Judeo-Christian Demon-God Satan was named. (Elements of the Greek nature deities known as satyrs, along with their horned, cloven-hoofed leader Pan, were also appended to the Christian figure of Satan, or the Devil, as he is also known.)

SCOTIA: the Celtic Ancestor-Goddess after whom Scotland and the Scottish people were named.

SIRENS: in Greek mythology, three goddess-women

who used their beautiful voices and music to lure sailors to certain doom on the rocky coasts of their island home. The Sirens gave us the words the Sirenusian Islands (located near modern day Paestum, Italy) and Sorrento (Italy), from the Greek word for Siren.

SKADI: the Celto-German Death-Goddess who gave her name to Scandinavia and the Scandinavian people, as well as to the Scottish island of Skye.

UNI: the Etruscan Creatrix-Mother-Goddess who gave her name to our Universe.

URD: the Scandinavian Goddess whose name became the word weird.

VENUS: the Roman Sex- and Love-Goddess who gave

her name to the city of Venice, Italy, and who also provided us with the words venerate, venereal, venison, and venery.

Thousands more of such goddesses could be listed. Many of the world's most famous mountains and mountain ranges, such as the Himalayas, for example, were named after female deities.

Even many common female first names derive from female deities. The following is a brief list of examples:

Abigail, Anna, Anne, Aurora, Bridget, Brigid, Camilla, Candace, Candi, Cassandra, Cassiopeia, Chloë, Claudia, Deborah, Deirdre, Diane, Diana, Dinah, Dionne, Doris, Daphne, Esther, Eve, Felicity, Grace, Guinevere, Gwen, Hannah, Helen, Ida, Irene, Iris, Jocasta, Judith,

Kelly/Kelle, Leah, Lisa, Lilian, Lolita, Lucinda, Lucy, Marcia, Maria, Mary, Maya, Melissa, Miriam, Morgan, Pandora, Penelope, Phyllis, Rachel, Rebecca, Rhea, Rhiannon, Sarah, Selene, Sheila, Suki, Sybil, Thea, Vivian, and Virginia.

If you are in need of a Goddess name for your newborn daughter this list is a good place to begin.

3

Kelle: The Blessed Lady of Ireland

EVERY GODDESS MENTIONED in the foregoing chapter is merely an aspect and a cultural personification of the One Great Goddess, the Earth-Mother, the Virgin-Mother, the Moon-Mother, who among the matrifocal Celts was known as Kelle.

Celtic though she was, etymology tells us that Kelle had her beginnings in Asia, where she existed from prehistoric times as the "Dark Mother," a Triple-Goddess (the original Holy Trinity) known in India as Kali Ma, Kali Mari, or simply Kali.

Down through the ages Kali was adopted by untold cultures, such as the Saxons, who knew her as Kale; the Finns who called her Kalma; the Nordics who called her Kelda or Kilda; and the early Britons who referred to this enigmatic deity as Black Annis.

The Goddess-worshiping Spaniards knew her as Califia, which is why they named one of their newly discovered lands after her: California, meaning "the Land Bestowed by the Goddess Califia (or Cali)."

It was among the Celtic tribes, however, where she was known as Kelle, that her most ardent admirers were to be found. Indeed, so great was their love for her that they even named themselves after her: the Kelts or Celts, meaning "the followers of the Goddess Kelle."

Like other societies, the Celts too have personified this Goddess in many different forms. The Scots call her *Cailleach Bheur* ("Hag of Winter") or Carlin ("Old Woman"); in Northern Ireland she is the hag-spirit of the lakes, Cally Berry; in the Irish Republic she is the "Old Gloomy Woman" known as the Hag of Beare; while on the Isle of Man she is *Cailleach Ny Groamch*.

In the old matricentric Celtic religion, Kelle's divine essence was referred to as *Kele-De* (the "Spirit of the Goddess Kelle"), while her cave shrines (symbols of her magical womb) were known as *Kill* (that is, "caves" or "cells").

One of her major temple sites in west-central Ireland retains her memory in its Celtic-Viking name: Kildare, "the city of the Goddess Kelda," which like all of Kelle's shrines, was strictly off limits to men.

In stark contrast to masculine religions, which stress obedience to rigid moral codes and external rules in order to reach Heaven, Kelle places emphasis on attaining enlightenment by way of a personal inner journey, through such practices as fasting, kindness, generosity, good deeds, and most importantly, prayer and meditation.

Thus her Celtic followers are often portrayed in ancient art sitting in the Lotus Position, earnestly seeking "the Queendom of Goddess" within (male religions later borrowed and masculinized many of Goddess' teachings;

see, for example, Luke 17:20-21).

Far from being a "dead Pagan deity, old and forgotten," Kelle lives on, more vital than ever. Not only is she still openly venerated and honored by many modern day Celts (and even by some non-Celts), but her name survives in the contemporary surname Kelly (and its countless variations, such as Kelley, Kellie, O'Kelly, and MacKelly).

Indeed, those who possess the last name Kelly can proudly trace their ancestry to this, the original and all-powerful Celtic Supreme Being, whose name in Irish Gaelic means "Warrior-Maiden."

Even Christians continue to unwittingly pay homage to this mighty Pagan Goddess, the Celtic version of the world's first Supreme Being. Like her Hindu counterpart Kali Mari, Kelle was also known as Keli-Mary, another one of the many Goddess prototypes upon which the figure of the Virgin Mary was later modeled.

This makes Kelle, not Mary, the original "Blessed Lady of Ireland," the name by which she is still known to Celtic poets.

The Celtic worship of Kelle has always been an enduring one, which is why the early Christian Fathers found it impossible to suppress her. The solution, one that the Church used with most other Pagan deities as well, was to adopt, assimilate, and christianize her. Thus was born the fictitious Christian holy woman "Saint Kilda," said to have dwelt on "Saint Kilda's Isle."

Semantic obfuscation, however, cannot conceal the island's original name and true nature: Kelle's Isle, one more of the Celtic Goddess' early sacred sites, where only women were allowed to set foot.

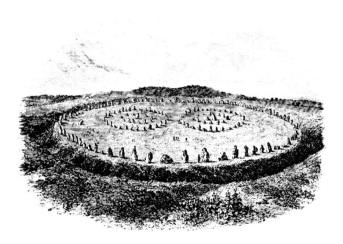

Ancient Anglo-Celtic monuments at Avebury, Wiltshire, England, symbolizing, in part, the female breasts and pregnant abdomen of the Great Mother-Goddess, possibly of Kelle, or perhaps her British counterpart Bride, Brigantia, or Britannia. The circular structures contain lunar (and possibly solar) symbolism and sacred numerology as well.

Bibliography

Adler, Margot. *Drawing Down the Moon*. Boston, MA: Beacon Press, 1981.

Albright, William Powell. *Yahweh and the Gods of Canaan*. New York, NY: Doubleday, 1968.

Allen, Paula Gunn. *The Sacred Hoop: Recovering the Feminine in American Indian Traditions*. Boston, MA: Beacon Press, 1986.

Allison, Dale C., Jr. *Resurrecting Jesus: The Earliest Christian Tradition and Its Interpreters*. New York, NY: T and T Clark, 2005.

Andrews, Ted. *The Occult Christ: Angelic Mysteries, Seasonal Rituals, and the Divine Feminine*. St. Paul, MN: Llewellyn, 1993.

Angus, Samuel. *The Mystery-Religions and Christianity: A Study of the Religious Background of Early Christianity*. 1925. New York, NY: Citadel Press, 1966 ed.

Ardrey, Robert. *African Genesis*. 1961. New York, NY: Dell, 1972 ed.

——. *The Territorial Imperative*. 1966. New York, NY: Delta, 1968 ed.

Armstrong, Karen. *A History of God: The 4000-Year Quest of Judaism,*

Christianity and Islam. New York, NY: Knopf, 1993.

Ashe, Geoffrey. *The Virgin: Mary's Cult and the Re-emergence of the Goddess*. 1976. London, UK: Arkana, 1988 ed.

———. *Dawn Behind the Dawn: A Search for the Earthly Paradise*. New York, NY: Henry Holt, 1992.

Atkins, Gaius Glenn, and Charles Samuel Braden. *Procession of the Gods*. 1930. New York, NY: Harper and Brothers Publishers, 1936 ed.

Attwater, Donald. *The Penguin Dictionary of Saints*. 1965. Harmondsworth, UK: Penguin, 1983 ed.

Avalon, Arthur. *Shakti and Shakta*. New York, NY: Dover, 1978.

Ayto, John. *Dictionary of Word Origins*. New York, NY: Arcade, 1990.

Bachofen, Johann Jakob. *Myth, Religion and Mother Right*. Princeton, NJ: Princeton University Press, 1967.

Baigent, Michael. *The Jesus Papers: Exposing the Greatest Cover-Up in History*. San Francisco, CA: Harper San Francisco, 2006.

Baigent, Michael, and Richard Leigh. *The Dead Sea Scrolls Deception*. 1991. New York, NY: Touchstone, 1993 ed.

Baigent, Michael, Richard Leigh, and Henry Lincoln. *Holy Blood,*

Holy Grail. 1982. New York, NY: Dell, 1983. ed.

———. *The Messianic Legacy*. New York, NY: Dell, 1986.

Baring, Anne, and Jules Cashford. *The Myth of the Goddess: Evolution of an Image*. 1991. Harmondsworth, UK: Arkana, 1993 ed.

Baring-Gould, Sabine. *Curious Myths of the Middle Ages*. New York, NY: University Books, 1967.

Barnstone, Willis (ed.). *The Other Bible: Ancient Esoteric Texts*. New York, NY: Harper and Row, 1984.

Baroja, Julio Caro. *The World of Witches*. Chicago, IL: University of Chicago Press, 1965.

Bauvel, Robert, and Adrian Gilbert. *The Orion Mystery: Unlocking the Secrets of the Pyramids*. New York, NY: Three Rivers Press, 1995.

Bayley, Harold. *Archaic England: An Essay in Deciphering Prehistory From Megalithic Monuments, Earthworks, Customs, Coins, Place-names, and Faerie Superstitions*. London, UK: Chapman and Hall, 1920.

Begg, Ean. *The Cult of the Black Virgin*. Harmondsworth, UK: Arkana, 1985.

Bell, Robert E. *Women of Classical Mythology: A Biographical Dictionary*.

1991. Oxford, UK: Oxford University Press, 1993 ed.

Besant, Annie. *Esoteric Christianity or the Lesser Mysteries*. London, UK: Theosophical Publishing Society, 1905.

Best, Robert M. *Noah's Ark and the Ziusudra Epic: Sumerian Origins of the Flood Myth*. Fort Myers, FL: Enlil Press, 1999.

Bhagavad Gita (Juan Mascaró, trans.). c. 500 BC. Harmondsworth, UK: Penguin, 1962.

Bierlein, John Francis. *Parallel Myths*. New York, NY: Ballantine Wellspring, 1994.

Binder, Pearl. *Magic Symbols of the World*. London, UK: Hamlyn, 1972.

Boardman, John, Jasper Griffin, and Oswyn Murray (eds.). *The Roman World*. 1986. Oxford, UK: Oxford University Press, 1988 ed.

Boates, Karen Scott (ed.). *The Goddess Within*. Philadelphia, PA: Running Press, 1990.

Bouquet, Alan Coates. *Comparative Religion: A Survey and Comparison of the Great Religions of the World*. London, UK: Penguin, 1942.

Bowden, John. *Archaeology and the Bible*. Austin, TX: American

Atheist Press, 1982.

Branston, Brian. *Gods of the North*. London, UK: Thames and Hudson, 1955.

Bratton, Fred Gladstone. *Myths and Legends of the Ancient Near East: Great Stories of the Sumero-Akkadian, Egyptian, Ugaritic-Canaanite, and Hittite Cultures*. New York, NY: Thomas Y. Crowell, 1970.

Breasted, James Henry. *Ancient Records of Egypt*. 5 vols. Chicago: IL: University of Chicago Press, 1906.

Brewster, Harold Pomeroy. *Saints and Festivals of the Christian Church*. New York, NY: Frederick A. Stokes, 1904.

Briffault, Robert Stephen. *The Mothers: The Matriarchal Theory of Social Origins*. 1927. New York, NY: Macmillan, 1931 (single volume, abridged) ed.

Briggs, Katherine. *The Vanishing People: Fairy Lore and Legends*. New York, NY: Pantheon, 1978.

Brownrigg, Ronald. *Who's Who in the New Testament*. 1971. New York, NY: Oxford University Press, 1993 ed.

Bucke, Richard Maurice. *Cosmic Consciousness: A Study in the Evolution of the Human Mind*. 1901. New York, NY: Dutton, 1969 ed.

Budapest, Zsuzsanna Emese. *The Holy Book of Women's Mysteries* (Part 1). 1979. Oakland, CA: Susan B. Anthony Coven No. 1, 1982 ed.

——. *The Holy Book of Women's Mysteries* (Part 2). Oakland, CA: Susan B. Anthony Coven No. 1, 1980.

Budge, Ernest Alfred Wallis. *Egyptian Magic*. London, UK: Kegan, Paul, Trench, Trübner, and Co., 1901.

——. *Osiris and the Egyptian Resurrection*. Vol. 1. London, UK: Philip Lee Warner, 1911.

——. *Amulets and Talismans*. 1930. New York, NY: Citadel, 1992 ed.

Bulfinch, Thomas. *Bulfinch's Mythology: The Age of Fable, the Age of Chivalry, Legends of Charlemagne*. New York, NY: Thomas Y. Crowell, 1913.

Bullough, Vern L., and Bonnie Bullough. *The Subordinate Sex: A History of Attitudes Toward Women*. 1973. Baltimore, MD: Penguin, 1974 ed.

——. *Women and Prostitution: A Social History*. 1978. Buffalo, NY: Prometheus, 1987 ed.

Caesar, Gaius Julius. *The Conquest of Gaul* [*Gallic War*] (S. A. Handford, trans.). 51 BC. Harmondsworth, UK: Penguin,

1951, 1988 ed.

Calasso, Roberto. *The Marriage of Cadmus and Harmony* (Tim Parks, trans.). New York, NY: Alfred A. Knopf, 1993.

Calvocoressi, Peter. *Who's Who in the Bible.* 1987. Harmondsworth, UK: Penguin, 1990 ed.

Campanelli, Pauline. *Ancient Ways: Reclaiming Pagan Traditions.* 1991. St. Paul, MN: Llewellyn, 1992 ed.

Campbell, Joseph. *The Masks of God: Primitive Mythology.* Vol. 1. 1959. Harmondsworth, UK: Arkana, 1991 ed.

——. *The Masks of God: Oriental Mythology.* Vol. 2. 1962. Harmondsworth, UK: Arkana, 1991 ed.

Carlyon, Richard. *A Guide to the Gods: An Essential Guide to World Mythology.* New York, NY: Quill, 1981.

Carpenter, Edward. *Pagan and Christian Creeds: Their Origin and Meaning*: New York, NY: Blue Ribbon, 1920.

Carson, Anne. *Goddesses and Wise Women: The Literature of Feminist Spirituality, An Annotated Bibliography* (1980-1992). Freedom, CA: Crossing Press, 1992.

Carter, Jesse Benedict. *The Religious Life of Ancient Rome: A Study in the Development of Religious Consciousness, From the Foundation of the City Until the Death of Gregory the Great.* Boston, MA: Houghton Mifflin, 1911.

Cassius, Dio. *The Roman History: The Reign of Augustus* (Ian Scott-Kilvert, trans.). C. 214-226. Harmondsworth, UK: Penguin, 1988.

Cavendish, Richard. *A History of Magic.* 1987. Harmondsworth, UK: Arkana, 1990 ed.

Christie-Murray, David. *A History of Heresy.* Oxford, UK: Oxford University Press, 1976.

Cirlot, J. E. *A Dictionary of Symbols.* 1962. New York, NY: Philosophical Library, 1983 ed.

Collins, Sheila D. *A Different Heaven and Earth: A Feminist Perspective on Religion.* Valley Forge, PA: Judson Press, 1974.

Comay, Joan. *Who's Who in the Old Testament (Together with the Apocrypha).* 1971. New York, NY: Oxford University Press, 1993 ed.

Condon, R. J. *Our Pagan Christmas.* Austin, TX: American Atheist Press, 1989.

Cotterell, Arthur. *A Dictionary of World Mythology.* 1979. New York, NY: Oxford University Press, 1990 ed.

———. *The Macmillan Illustrated Encyclopedia of Myths and Legends*. New York, NY: Macmillan, 1989.

Cross, Frank L., and Elizabeth A. Livingstone. *The Oxford Dictionary of the Christian Church*. 1957. London, UK: Oxford University Press, 1974 ed.

Crossley-Holland, Kevin. *The Norse Myths*. New York, NY: Pantheon, 1980.

Cumont, Franz Valéry Marie. *The Mysteries of Mithra*. New York, NY: Dover, 1956.

———. *Oriental Religions in Roman Paganism*. New York, NY: Dover, 1956.

———. *Astrology and Religion Among the Greeks and Romans*. New York, NY: Dover, 1960.

Dalley, Stephanie (trans.). *Myths From Mesopotamia: Creation, the Flood, Gilgamesh, and Others*. 1989. Oxford, UK: Oxford University Press, 2008 ed.

Daly, Mary. *Beyond God the Father: Toward a Philosophy of Women's Liberation*. Boston, MA: Beacon Press, 1973.

———. *Gyn/ecology: The Metaethics of Radical Feminism*. Boston, MA: Beacon Press, 1978.

Davidson, Gustav. *A Dictionary of Angels*. 1967. New York, NY: The Free Press, 1971 ed.

Davidson, Hilda Roderick Ellis. *Gods and Myths of Northern Europe*. 1964. London, UK: Penguin, 1990 ed.

——. *Pagan Scandinavia*. New York, NY: Frederick A. Praeger, 1967.

——. *Gods and Myths of the Viking Age*. New York, NY: Bell, 1981.

——. *Myths and Symbols in Pagan Europe: Early Scandinavian and Celtic Religions*. Syracuse, NY: Syracuse University Press, 1988.

Davis, John J. *Biblical Numerology: A Basic Study of the Use of Numbers in the Bible*. 1968. Grand Rapids, MI: Baker Book House, 1988 ed.

Delaney, John J. *Pocket Dictionary of Saints*. 1980. New York, NY: Image, 1983 (abridged) ed.

Delehaye, Hippolyte. *The Legends of the Saints: An Introduction to Hagiography*. New York, NY: Fordham University Press, 1962.

Dennis, Rabbi Geoffrey W. *The Encyclopedia of Jewish Myth, Magic and Mysticism*. Woodbury, MN: Llewellyn, 2007.

de Volney, Constantin François. *The Ruins, or, A Survey of the*

Revolutions of Empires. 1791. London, UK: James Watson, 1857 ed.

de Voragine, Jacobus. *The Golden Legend, or Lives of the Saints.* 7 vols. C. 1260. London, UK: J. M. Dent and Co., 1900.

Didron, M. *Christian Iconography; or, The History of Christian Art in the Middle Ages.* 2 vols. London, UK: Henry G. Bohn, 1851.

Dione, R. L. *Is God Supernatural?: The 4,000-Year Misunderstanding.* New York, NY: Bantam, 1976.

Doane, Thomas William. *Bible Myths and Their Parallels in Other Religions.* New York, NY: University Books, 1971.

Downing, Christine. *The Goddess: Mythological Images of the Feminine.* New York, NY: Crossroads Publishing, 1984.

Eban, Abba. *Heritage: Civilization and the Jews.* New York, NY: Summit, 1984.

Egyptian Book of the Dead, The (E. A. Wallis Budge, trans.). 1895. New York, NY: Dover Publications, 1967 ed.

Eisler, Riane. *The Chalice and the Blade: Our History, Our Future.* New York, NY: Perennial, 1987.

Elder, Dorothy. *From Metaphysical to Mystical: A Study of the Way.* Denver, CO: Doriel Publishing Co., 1992.

Eliade, Mircea. *A History of Religious Ideas: From Gautama Buddha to the Triumph of Christianity* (Willard R. Trask, trans.). Vol. 2. 1978. Chicago, IL: The University of Chicago Press, 1982 ed.

Eliot, Alexander. *The Universal Myths: Heroes, Gods, Tricksters, and Others.* New York, NY: Meridian, 1976.

Ellis, Peter Berresford. *A Dictionary of Irish Mythology.* 1987. Oxford, UK: Oxford University Press, 1992 ed.

Encyclopedia Britannica: A New Survey of Universal Knowledge. 1768. Chicago/London, UK: Encyclopedia Britannica, 1955 ed.

Evans, Bergen. *Dictionary of Mythology.* 1970. New York, NY: Laurel, 1991 ed.

Evans, Elizabeth Edson. *The Christ Myth: A Study.* New York, NY: Truth Seeker Co., 1900.

Farmer, David Hugh. *The Oxford Dictionary of Saints.* 1978. Oxford, UK: Oxford University Press, 1992 ed.

Farrell, Deborah, and Carole Presser (eds.). *The Herder Symbol Dictionary: Symbols from Art, Archaeology, Mythology, Literature, and Religion* (Boris Matthews, trans.). 1978. Wilmette, IL: Chiron, 1990 ed.

Fideler, David. *Jesus Christ, Sun of God: Ancient Cosmology and Early Christian Symbolism*. Wheaton, IL: Quest, 1993.

Fillmore, Charles, and Theodosia DeWitt Schobert. *Metaphysical Bible Dictionary*. Unity Village, MO: Unity School of Christianity, 1931.

Finegan, Jack. *Light from the Ancient Past: The Archaeological Background of the Hebrew-Christian Religion* (Vol. 1). 1946. Princeton, NJ: Princeton University Press, 1974 ed.

Finger, Ben, Jr. *Concise World History*. New York, NY: Philosophical Library, 1959.

Fischer, Carl. *The Myth and Legend of Greece*. Dayton, OH: George A. Pflaum, 1968.

Forrest, M. Isidora. *Offering to Isis: Knowing the Goddess Through Her Sacred Symbols*. St. Paul, MN: Llewellyn, 2005.

Fox, Matthew. *The Coming of the Cosmic Christ: The Healing of Mother Earth and the Birth of a Global Renaissance*. New York, NY: Harper and Row, 1988.

——. (ed.) *Western Spirituality: Historical Roots, Ecumenical Routes*. Santa Fe, NM: Bear and Co., 1981.

Fox, Robin Lane. *Pagans and Christians*. New York, NY: Knopf,

1986.

——. *The Unauthorized Version: Truth and Fiction in the Bible.* New York, NY: Knopf, 1991.

Frazer, Sir James George. *The Golden Bough: A Study in Magic and Religion.* 1922. New York, NY: Collier, 1963 (abridged) ed.

——. *Folklore in the Old Testament.* New York, NY: Tudor Publishing, (abridged) 1923.

Freke, Timothy, and Peter Grandy. *The Jesus Mysteries: Was the Original Jesus a Pagan God?* New York, NY: Three Rivers Press, 1999.

——. *Jesus and the Lost Goddess: The Secret Teachings of the Original Christians.* New York, NY: Three Rivers Press, 2002.

Freud, Sigmund. *Totem and Taboo.* 1918. New York, NY: Vintage, 1946 ed.

——. *The Future of an Illusion.* 1928. New York, NY: W. W. Norton, 1961 ed.

——. *New Introductory Lectures Psychoanalysis.* Lecture no. 35: "A Philosophy of Life," 1932.

Gantz, Jeffrey (trans.). *Early Irish Myths and Sagas.* 1981. Harmondsworth, UK: Penguin, 1988 ed.

Gelling, Peter, and Hilda Ellis Davidson. *The Chariot of the Sun and Other Rites and Symbols of the Northern Bronze Age*. New York, NY: Frederick A. Praeger, 1969.

Gimbutas, Marija Alseikaitė. *The Civilization of the Goddess: The World of Old Europe* (Joan Marler, ed.). New York, NY: Harper Collins, 1991.

——. *The Goddesses and Gods of Old Europe: Myths and Cult Images.* 1974. Berkeley, CA: University of California Press, 1992 ed.

Goldenberg, Naomi. *The Changing of the Gods: Feminism and the End of Traditional Religions*. Boston, MA: Beacon Press, 1979.

Gordon, Richard Stuart. *The Encyclopedia of Myths and Legends*. 1993. London, UK: Headline, 1994 ed.

Goring, Rosemary (ed.). *Larousse Dictionary of Beliefs and Religions*. 1992. Edinburgh, Scotland: Larousse, 1995 ed.

Graves, Kersey. *The World's Sixteen Crucified Saviors, or, Christianity Before Christianity: Containing New, Startling, and Extraordinary Revelations in Religious History, which Disclose the Oriental Origin of All the Doctrines, Principles, Precepts, and Miracles of the Christian New Testament, and Furnishing a Key for Unlocking*

THE BOOK OF KELLE

Many of Its Sacred Mysteries, Besides Comprising the History of Sixteen Heathen Crucified Gods. Boston, MA: Colby and Rich, 1876.

Graves, Robert. *The Greek Myths.* 1955. Harmondsworth, UK: Penguin, 1992 combined ed.

——. *The White Goddess: A Historical Grammar of Poetic Myth.* 1948. New York, NY: Noonday Press, 1991 ed.

Graves, Robert, and Raphael Patai. *Hebrew Myths: The Book of Genesis.* 1964. New York, NY: Anchor, 1989 ed.

Gray, John. *Near Eastern Mythology: Mesopotamia, Syria, and Palestine.* London, UK: Hamlyn, 1963.

Greenberg, Gary. *101 Myths of the Bible: How Ancient Scribes Invented Biblical History.* Naperville, IL: Sourcebooks, 2000.

Grimal, Pierre. *The Penguin Dictionary of Classical Mythology* (A. R. Maxwell-Hyslop, trans.). 1951. Harmondsworth, UK: Penguin, 1990 ed.

Grotjahn, Martin. *The Voice of the Symbol.* Los Angeles, CA: Mara Books, 1971.

Guthrie, William K. C. *The Greeks and Their Gods.* Boston, MA: Beacon Press, 1955.

Hadas, Moses (ed.). *A History of Rome*. Garden City, NY: Doubleday Anchor, 1956.

Haining, Peter. *Witchcraft and Black Magic*. New York, NY: Grosset and Dunlap, 1972.

Hall, Eleanor L. *The Moon and the Virgin: Reflections on the Archetypal Feminine*. New York, NY: Harper and Row, 1980.

Hall, John Richard Clark. *A Concise Anglo-Saxon Dictionary*. 1894. Toronto, Canada: University of Toronto Press (and the Medieval Academy of America), 1960 ed. (1996 imprint).

Hall, Manly P. *The Secret Teachings of All Ages*. 1925. Los Angeles, CA: The Philosophical Research Society, 1989 ed.

Halliday, William Reginald. *Greek and Roman Folklore*. New York, NY: Cooper Square, 1963.

Hamilton, Edith. *The Greek Way*. 1930. New York, NY: Mentor, 1959 ed.

——. *The Roman Way*. 1932. New York, NY: Mentor, 1961 ed.

——. *Mythology: Timeless Tales of Gods and Heroes*. 1940. New York, NY: Mentor, 1963 ed.

Harrison, Michael. *The Roots of Witchcraft*. Secaucus, NJ: Citadel Press, 1974.

Haskins, Susan. *Mary Magdalene: Myth and Metaphor.* New York, NY: Harcourt Brace and Co., 1993.

Heidel, Alexander. *The Gilgamesh Epic and Old Testament Parallels.* Chicago, IL: University of Chicago Press, 1949.

Heindel, Max. *Nature Spirits and Nature Forces.* Oceanside, CA: Rosicrucian Fellowship, 1937.

Herm, Gerhard. *The Celts: The People Who Came Out of the Darkness.* New York, NY: St. Martin's Press, 1976.

Hinnells, John R. (ed.). *Persian Mythology.* London, UK: Hamlyn, 1973.

———. *The Penguin Dictionary of Religions: From Abraham to Zoroaster.* 1984. Harmondsworth, UK: Penguin, 1986 ed.

Hodson, Geoffrey. *The Hidden Wisdom in the Holy Bible.* Vol. 1. 1967. Wheaton, IL: Quest, 1978 ed.

———. *The Hidden Wisdom in the Holy Bible.* Vol. 2. 1967. Wheaton, IL: Quest, 1978 ed.

Hoeller, Stephan A. *Jung and the Lost Gospels: Insights into the Dead Sea Scrolls and the Nag Hammadi Library.* 1989. Wheaton, IL: Quest, 1990 ed.

Holroyd, Stuart. *The Arkana Dictionary of New Perspectives.*

Harmondsworth, UK: Arkana, 1989.

Hooke, S. K. *Middle Eastern Mythology: From the Assyrians to the Hebrews*. 1963. Harmondsworth, UK: Penguin, 1991 ed.

Hopfe, Lewis M. *Religions of the World*. 1976. New York, NY: Macmillan, 1987 ed.

Hoyland, Robert G. *Arabia and the Arabs: From the Bronze Age to the Coming of Islam*. London, UK: Routledge, 2001.

Hutchinson, Richard Wyatt. *Prehistoric Crete*. 1962. Harmondsworth, UK: Penguin, 1968 ed.

Hutton, Ronald. *The Pagan Religions of the Ancient British Isles: Their Nature and Legacy*. 1991. Oxford, UK: Blackwell, 2000 ed.

Huxley, Francis. *The Way of the Sacred*. New York, NY: Doubleday, 1974.

Ide, Arthur Frederick. *Yahweh's Wife: Sex in the Evolution of Monotheism (A Study of Yahweh, Asherah, Ritual Sodomy and Temple Prostitution)*. Las Colinas, TX: Monument Press, 1991.

Jackson, John G. *Christianity Before Christ*. Austin, TX: American Atheist Press, 1985.

Johnson, Robert A. *She: Understanding Feminine Psychology*. 1976.

New York, NY: Perennial, 1977 ed.

Jonas, Hans. *The Gnostic Religion: The Message of the Alien God and the Beginnings of Christianity*. 1958. Boston, MA: Beacon Press, 2001 ed.

Jones, Gwyn. *A History of the Vikings*. 1968. Oxford, UK: Oxford University Press, 1984 ed.

Jones, Prudence, and Nigel Pennick. *A History of Pagan Europe*. London, UK: Routledge, 1995.

Jung, Carl Gustav. *Man and his Symbols*. 1964. New York, NY: Dell, 1968 ed.

Kirk, G. S. *The Nature of the Greek Myths*. 1974. Harmondsworth, UK: Penguin, 1978 ed.

Klein, Peter (ed.). *The Catholic Source Book*. Dubuque, IA: Brown-Roa, 2000.

Knight, Richard Payne. *A Discourse On the Worship of Priapus, and Its Connection With the Mystic Theology of the Ancients*. London, UK: privately printed, 1865 ed.

——. *The Symbolic Language of Ancient Art and Mythology*. New York, NY: J. W. Bouton, 1892.

Kramer, Heinrich, and Jakob Sprenger. *Malleus Maleficarum*. 1486.

New York, NY: Dover, 1971.

Kramer, Samuel Noah. *History Begins at Sumer: Thirty-Nine Firsts in Recorded History*. 1956. Philadelphia, PA: University of Pennsylvania Press, 1981 ed.

Kuhn, Alvin Boyd. *A Rebirth for Christianity*. 1970. Wheaton, IL: Quest, 2005.

Lacy, Norris J. (ed.). *The Arthurian Encyclopedia*. New York, NY: Garland Publishing, 1986.

Laistner, Max Ludwig Wolfram. *Christianity and Pagan Culture in the Later Roman Empire*. Ithaca, NY: Cornell University Press, 1951.

Lamsa, George M. *The Holy Bible: From Ancient Eastern Manuscripts*. 1933. Philadelphia, PA: A. J. Holman, 1968 ed.

Larousse Encyclopedia of Mythology, New. 1959. London, UK: Hamlyn, 1976 ed.

Layton, Bentley. *The Gnostic Scriptures: Ancient Wisdom for the New Age*. 1987. New York, NY: Anchor, 1995 ed.

Leakey, Richard E., and Roger Lewin. *Origins Reconsidered: In Search of What Makes Us Human*. New York, NY: Doubleday, 1992.

Leeming, David Adams. *The World of Myth*. 1990. Oxford, UK:

Oxford University Press, 1992 ed.

Legge, Francis. *Forerunners and Rivals of Christianity*. 2 vols. New York, NY: University Books, 1964.

LeLoup, Jean-Yves. *The Gospel of Mary Magdalene*. Rochester, VT: Inner Traditions, 2002.

———. *The Gospel of Philip: Jesus, Mary Magdalene, and the Gnosis of Sacred Union*. Rochester, VT: Inner Traditions, 2004.

———. *The Gospel of Thomas: The Gnostic Wisdom of Jesus*. Rochester, VT: Inner Traditions, 2005.

Lerner, Gerda. *The Creation of Patriarchy*. 1986. Oxford, UK: Oxford University Press, 1987 ed.

Levi. *The Aquarian Gospel of Jesus the Christ: The Philosophic and Practical Basis of the Religion of the Aquarian Age of the World and of the Church Universal*. Marina Del Ray, CA: DeVorss and Co., 1982.

Lewis, Harvey Spencer. *Mansions of the Soul: The Cosmic Conception*. 1930. San Jose, CA: Ancient Mystical Order Rosae Crucis (AMORC), 1969 ed.

Lindsay, Jack. *The Origins of Astrology*. New York, NY: Barnes and Noble, 1971.

Littleton, C. Scott (ed). *Mythology: The Illustrated Anthology of World Myth and Storytelling*. London, UK: Duncan Baird Publishers, 2002.

Lockyer, Herbert. *All the Women of the Bible*. Grand Rapids, MI: Zondervan, n.d.

Loetscher, Lefferts A. (ed.-in-chief). *Twentieth Century Encyclopedia of Religious Knowledge*. 2 vols. Grand Rapids, MI: Baker Book House, 1955.

Ludlow, Daniel H. (ed.). *Encyclopedia of Mormonism: The History, Scripture, Doctrine, and Procedure of the Church of Jesus Christ of Latter-Day Saints*. New York, NY: Macmillan, 1992.

Lurker, Manfred. *The Gods and Symbols of Ancient Egypt*. 1974. New York, NY: Thames and Hudson, 1984 ed.

———. *Dictionary of Gods and Goddesses, Devils and Demons* (G. L. Campbell, trans.). 1984. London, UK: Routledge, 1988 ed.

MacCana, Proinsias. *Celtic Mythology*. London, UK: Hamlyn, 1970.

MacLysaght, Edward. *The Surnames of Ireland*. 1985. Dublin, Ireland: Irish Academic Press, 1999 ed.

Malachi, Tau. *Gnosis of the Cosmic Christ: A Gnostic Christian Kabbalah*. St. Paul, MN: Llewellyn, 2005.

———. *Living Gnosis: A Practical Guide to Gnostic Christianity*. St. Paul, MN: Llewellyn, 2005.

———. *St. Mary Magdalene: The Gnostic Tradition of the Holy Bride*. St. Paul, MN: Llewellyn, 2006.

Mann, Nicholas R. *The Isle of Avalon: Sacred Mysteries of Arthur and Glastonbury*. London, UK: Green Magic, 2001.

Marcus, Rebecca B. *Prehistoric Cave Paintings*. New York, NY: Franklin Watts, 1968.

Markale, Jean. *Cathedral of the Black Madonna: The Druids and the Mysteries of Chartres*. Rochester, VT: Inner Traditions, 2004.

Maspero, Gaston. *Popular Stories of Ancient Egypt*. New York, NY: University Books, 1967.

Massey, Gerald. *The Historical Jesus, and the Mythical Christ: Natural Genesis and Typology of Equinoctial Christolatry*. 1883. New York, NY: Cosimo, 2006 ed.

———. *Ancient Egypt: The Light of the World*. 12 vols. London, UK: T. Fisher Unwin, 1907.

Matthews, Caitlín and John. *The Encyclopedia of Celtic Wisdom: A Celtic Shaman's Sourcebook*. Rockport, MA: Element, 1994.

Matthews, John. *The Winter Solstice: The Sacred Traditions of Christmas*.

Wheaton, IL: Quest, 2003.

McArthur, Tom (ed.). *The Oxford Companion to the English Language.* Oxford, UK: Oxford University Press, 1992.

McKenzie, John L. *Dictionary of the Bible.* New York, NY: Collier/Macmillan, 1965.

McKinsey, C. Dennis. *The Encyclopedia of Biblical Errancy.* Amherst, NY: Prometheus, 1995.

McLean, Adam (ed.). *A Treatise on Angel Magic: Magnum Opus Hermetic Sourceworks.* 1989. York Beach, ME: Weiser, 2006 ed.

Mead, George Robert Stow. *Thrice-Greatest Hermes: Studies in Hellenistic Theosophy and Gnosis.* London, UK: Theosophical Publishing Society, 1906.

——. *The Mysteries of Mithra.* London, UK: Theosophical Publishing Society, 1907.

Meurois-Givaudan, Anne and Daniel. *The Way of the Essenes: Christ's Hidden Life Remembered.* Rochester, VT: Destiny, 1992.

Meyers, Carol (gen. ed.). *Women in Scripture: A Dictionary of Named and Unnamed Women in the Hebrew Bible, the Apocryphal/Deuterocanonical Books, and the New Testament.* 2000. Grand Rapids, MI: William B. Eerdmans, 2001 ed.

Miller, Malcolm. *Chartres Cathedral*. New York, NY: Riverside Book Co., 1997.

Miller, Robert J. (ed.). *The Complete Gospels* (Annotated Scholars Version). Sonoma, CA: Polebridge Press, 1994.

Mills, A. D. *Oxford Dictionary of English Place-names.* 1991. Oxford, UK: Oxford University Press, 1998 ed.

Mollenkott, Virginia Ramey. *The Divine Feminine: The Biblical Imagery of God as Female.* New York, NY: Crossroad Publishing, 1993.

Monaghan, Patricia. *The Book of Goddesses and Heroines.* 1990. St. Paul, MN: Llewellyn, 1991 ed.

Morgan, Elaine. *The Descent of Woman.* 1972. New York, NY: Bantam, 1973 ed.

Montagu, Ashley. *The Natural Superiority of Women.* 1952. New York, NY: Collier, 1992 ed.

Neumann, Erich. *The Great Mother: An Analysis of the Archetype* (Ralph Manheim, trans.). New York, NY: Pantheon, 1955.

Newall, Venetia. *The Encyclopedia of Witchcraft and Magic.* A and W Visual Library, 1974.

Norton-Taylor, Duncan. *The Emergence of Man: The Celts.* New York,

NY: Time-Life, 1974.

O'Brien, Arthur. *Europe Before Modern Times: An Ancient and Medieval History*. 1940. Chicago, IL: Loyola University Press, 1943 ed.

Odent, Michael. *Water and Sexuality*. Harmondsworth, UK: Arkana, 1990.

O'Flaherty, Wendy Doniger. *Hindu Myths*. Harmondsworth, UK: Penguin, 1975.

Olson, Carl (ed.). *The Book of the Goddess, Past and Present: An Introduction to Her Religion*. New York, NY: Crossroad, 1983.

Orme, A. R. *Ireland* (from "The World's Landscapes" series, James M. Houston, ed). Chicago, IL: Aldine, 1970.

Osborne, John. *Britain*. New York, NY: Time-Life, 1963.

Oxford English Dictionary, The (compact edition, 2 vols.). 1928. Oxford, UK: Oxford University Press, 1979 ed.

Patai, Raphael. *The Hebrew Goddess*. 1967. Detroit, MI: Wayne State University Press, 1990 ed.

Pennick, Nigel. *The Pagan Book of Days: A Guide to the Festivals, Traditions, and Sacred Days of the Year*. Rochester, VT:

Destiny, 1992.

Pepper, Elizabeth, and John Wilcock. *Magical and Mystical Sites: Europe and the British Isles.* Grand Rapids, MI: Phanes Press, 1992.

Perowne, Stewart. *Roman Mythology.* 1969. Twickenham, UK: Newnes Books, 1986 ed.

Pinch, Geraldine. *Egyptian Mythology: A Guide to the Gods, Goddesses, and Traditions of Ancient Egypt.* Oxford, UK: Oxford University Press, 2004.

Prophet, Elizabeth Clare. *Mary Magdalene and the Divine Feminine: Jesus' Lost Teachings on Woman - How Orthodoxy Suppressed Jesus' Revolution for Woman and Invented Original Sin.* Gardiner, MT: Summit University Press, 2005.

Qualls-Corbett, Nancy. *The Sacred Prostitute: Eternal Aspect of the Feminine.* Toronto, Canada: Inner City Books, 1988.

Raftery, Barry. *Pagan Celtic Ireland: The Enigma of the Irish Iron Age.* London, UK: Thames and Hudson, 1994.

Reaney, P. H., and R. M. Wilson. *A Dictionary of English Surnames.* 1958. Oxford, UK: Oxford University Press, 1997 ed.

Reed, Ellen Cannon. *Circle of Isis: Ancient Egyptian Magic for Modern*

Witches. Franklin Lakes, NJ: Career Press, 2002.

Regula, deTraci. *The Mysteries of Isis: Her Worship and Magick.* 1995. St. Paul, MN: Llewellyn, 2001 ed.

Reilly, Patricia Lynn. *A God Who Looks Like Me: Discovering a Woman-Affirming Spirituality.* New York, NY: Ballantine, 1995.

Robertson, John M. *Christianity and Mythology.* London, UK: Watts and Co., 1900.

——. *A Short History of Christianity.* London, UK: Watts and Co., 1902.

——. *Pagan Christs: Studies in Comparative Hierology.* London, UK: Watts and Co., 1903.

——. *Pagan Christs.* 1966. New York, NY: Dorset Press, 1987 ed.

Rufus, Anneli S., and Kristan Lawson. *Goddess Sites: Europe.* New York, NY: Harper Collins, 1991.

Runes, Dagobert D. (ed.). *Dictionary of Judaism.* 1959. New York, NY: Citadel Press, 1991 ed.

Rutherford, Ward. *Celtic Mythology: The Nature and Influence of Celtic Myth—from Druidism to Arthurian Legend.* New York, NY: Sterling, 1990.

Salmonson, Jessica Amanda. *The Encyclopedia of Amazons: Women*

Warriors from Antiquity to the Modern Era. New York, NY: Paragon House, 1991.

Schwartz, Howard. *Gabriel's Palace: Jewish Mystical Tales.* New York, NY: Oxford University Press, 1993.

——. *Tree of Souls: The Mythology of Judaism.* Oxford, UK: Oxford University Press, 2004.

Scott, George Ryley. *Phallic Worship: A History of Sex and Sexual Rites.* London, UK: Senate, 1996.

Seabrook, Lochlainn. *The Goddess Dictionary of Words and Phrases: Introducing a New Core Vocabulary for the Women's Spirituality Movement.* 1997. Franklin, TN: Sea Raven Press, 2010 ed.

——. *Britannia Rules: Goddess-Worship in Ancient Anglo-Celtic Society - An Academic Look at the United Kingdom's Spiritual Matricentric Past.* 1999. Franklin, TN: Sea Raven Press, 2010 ed.

——. *Aphrodite's Trade: The Hidden History of Prostitution Unveiled.* Franklin, TN: Sea Raven Press, 2010.

——. *The Way of Holiness: The Evolution of Religion—From the Cave Bear Cult to Christianity.* Franklin, TN: Sea Raven Press, unpublished manuscript.

——. *The Goddess Encyclopedia of Secret Words, Names, and Places.*

Franklin, TN: Sea Raven Press, unpublished manuscript.

——. *Seabrook's Complete Encyclopedia of Deities*. Franklin, TN: Sea Raven Press, unpublished manuscript.

——. *The Unauthorized Encyclopedia of the Bible*. Franklin, TN: Sea Raven Press, unpublished manuscript.

——. *The Complete Dictionary of Christian Mythology*. Franklin, TN: Sea Raven Press, unpublished manuscript.

Seznec, Jean. *The Survival of the Pagan Gods*. Princeton, NJ: Princeton University Press, 1953.

Shah, Amina. *Arabian Fairy Tales*. London, UK: Octagon Press, 1989.

——. *Tales From the Bazaars of Arabia: Folk Stories From the Middle East*. London, UK: Octagon Press, 2002.

Shaw, Ian (ed.). *The Oxford History of Ancient Egypt*. 2000. Oxford, UK: Oxford University Press, 2002 ed.

Simons, Gerald. *Barbarian Europe* (from the *Great Ages of Man* series). New York, NY: Time-Life, 1968.

Sjöö, Monica, and Barbara Mor. *The Great Cosmic Mother: Rediscovering the Religion of the Earth*. New York, NY: Harper and Row, 1987.

Skelton, Robin, and Margaret Blackwood. *Earth, Air, Fire, Water: Pre-Christian and Pagan Elements in British Songs, Rhymes and Ballads.* Harmondsworth, UK: Arkana, 1990.

Smith, Lacey Baldwin. *This Realm of England: 1399 to 1688.* 1966. Lexington, MA: D. C. Heath and Co., 1983 ed.

Sobol, Donald J. *The Amazons of Greek Mythology.* Cranbury, NJ: A.S. Barnes and Co., 1972.

Spence, Lewis. *Ancient Egyptian Myths and Legends.* 1915. New York, NY: Dover, 1990 ed.

———. *An Encyclopedia of Occultism.* 1920. New York, NY: Citadel Press, 1993 ed.

———. *The History and Origins of Druidism.* 1949. New York, NY: Samuel Weiser, 1971 ed.

Starbird, Margaret. *The Goddess in the Gospels: Reclaiming the Sacred Feminine.* Rochester, VT: Bear and Co., 1998.

———. *Magdalene's Lost Legacy: Symbolic Numbers and the Sacred Union in Christianity.* Rochester, VT: Bear and Co., 2003.

Stark, Rodney. *Discovering God: The Origins of the Great Religions and the Evolution of Belief.* New York, NY: HarperCollins, 2007.

Stein, Diane. *The Goddess Book of Days.* 1988. Freedom, CA: The

Crossing Press, 1992 ed.

Stetkevych, Jaroslav. *Muhammad and the Golden Bough: Reconstructing Arabian Myth.* Bloomington, IN: Indiana University Press, 1996.

Stone, Merlin. *When God was a Woman.* San Diego, CA: Harvest, 1976.

———. *Ancient Mirrors of Womanhood: A Treasury of Goddess and Heroine Lore from Around the World.* 1979. Boston, MA: Beacon Press, 1990 ed.

Strachan, Gordon. *Chartres: Sacred Geometry, Sacred Space.* Edinburgh, Scotland: Floris Books, 2003.

Streep, Peg. *Sanctuaries of the Goddess: The Sacred Landscapes and Objects.* Boston, MA: Bullfinch Press, 1994.

Strong, James. *Strong's Exhaustive Concordance of the Bible.* 1890. Nashville, TN: Abingdon Press, 1975 ed.

Sturluson, Snorri. *The Prose Edda.* Berkeley, CA: University of California Press, 1954.

Sykes, Egerton. *Who's Who in Non-Classical Mythology* (Alan Kendall, ed.). 1952. New York, NY: Oxford University Press, 1993 ed.

The Epic of Gilgamesh (N. K. Sandars, ed.).   Circa 3000 BCE.
Harmondsworth, UK: Penguin, 1960 (1972 ed.).

The Fossil Record and Evolution.   Collected articles from *Scientific
American.* San Francisco, CA: W. H. Freeman and Co., 1982
ed.

The Golden Treasury of Myths and Legends (adapted by Anne Terry
White). New York, NY: Golden Press, 1959.

Thompson, James Westfall, and Edgar Nathaniel Johnson.   *An
Introduction to Medieval Europe: 300-1500.* New York, NY:
W. W. Norton, 1937.

Thorsten, Geraldine. *God Herself: The Feminine Roots of Astrology.*
New York, NY: Avon, 1981.

Trevelyan, George Macaulay. *History of England: Vol. 1, From the
Earliest Times to the Reformation.* 1926. Garden City, NY:
Anchor/Doubleday, 1952 ed.

Tripp, Edward. *History of England: Vol. 2, The Tudors and the Stuart
Era.* 1926. Garden City, NY: Anchor, 1952 ed.

——. *The Meridian Handbook of Classical Mythology.*   1970.
Harmondsworth, UK: Meridian, 1974 ed.

Turcan, Robert. *The Cults of the Roman Empire.* 1992. Oxford, UK:

Blackwell, 2000 ed.

Van De Microop, Marc. *A History of the Ancient Near East, ca. 3000-323 BC.* 2004. Oxford, UK: Blackwell, 2007 ed.

Vermaseren, Maarten J. *Cybele and Attis.* London, UK: Thames and Hudson, 1977.

Walker, Barbara G. *The Woman's Encyclopedia of Myths and Secrets.* San Francisco, CA: Harper and Row, 1983.

——. *The Crone: Woman of Age, Wisdom, and Power.* San Francisco, CA: Harper and Row, 1985.

——. *The Woman's Dictionary of Symbols and Sacred Objects.* San Francisco, CA: Harper and Row, 1988.

Walum, Laurel Richardson. *The Dynamics of Sex and Gender: A Sociological Perspective.* Chicago, IL: Rand McNally College Publishing, 1977.

Watts, Alan. *Behold the Spirit: A Study in the Necessity of Mystical Religion.* 1947. New York, NY: Random House, 1971 ed.

Way, George, and Romilly Squire. *Scottish Clan and Family Encyclopedia.* Glasgow, Scotland: Harper Collins, 1994.

Weigall, Arthur. *The Life and Times of Akhnaton: Pharaoh of Egypt.* London, UK: W. Blackwood and Sons, 1910.

——. *Wanderings in Anglo-Saxon Britain*. New York, NY: George H. Doran, 1926.

——. *The Paganism in Our Christianity*. New York, NY: G. P. Putnam's Sons, 1928.

White, Jon Manchip. *Ancient Egypt: Its Culture and History*. 1952. New York, NY: Dover, 1970 ed.

——. *Everyday Life in Ancient Egypt*. 1963. New York, NY: Perigree, 1980 ed.

White, R. J. *The Horizon Concise History of England*. New York, NY: American Heritage, 1971.

Wilde, Lady. *Irish Cures, Mystic Charms, and Superstitions* (compiled by Sheila Anne Barry). New York, NY: Sterling Publishing, 1991.

Wilkinson, Richard H. *The Complete Temples of Ancient Egypt*. London, UK: Thames and Hudson, 2000.

——. *The Complete Gods and Goddesses of Ancient Egypt*. London, UK: Thames and Hudson, 2003.

Wind, Edgar. *Pagan Mysteries in the Renaissance*. New York, NY: W. W. Norton, 1968.

Winks, Robin W., Crane Brinton, John B. Christopher, and Robert

Lee Wolff. *A History of Civilization, Vol. 1: Prehistory to 1715.* 1955. Englewood Cliffs, NJ: Prentice Hall, 1988 ed.

Witt, Reginald Eldred. *Isis in the Ancient World.* 1971. Baltimore, MD: John Hopkins University Press, 1997.

Young, Dudley. *Origins of the Sacred: The Ecstasies of Love and War.* 1991. New York, NY: Harper Perennial, 1992 ed.

Young, G. Douglas (gen. ed.). *Young's Compact Bible Dictionary.* 1984. Wheaton, IL: Tyndale House, 1989 ed.

Zaehner, R. C. (ed.) *Encyclopedia of the World's Religions.* 1959. New York, NY: Barnes and Noble, 1997 ed.

Zimmerman, J. E. *Dictionary of Classical Mythology.* New York, NY: Bantam, 1964.

An ancient Celtic cromlech, or altar.

Index

About the Author

LOCHLAINN SEABROOK is an unreconstructed Southern author and traditional agrarian of Scottish, Irish, Welsh, German, and English extraction. An encyclopedist and lexicographer, an artist, graphic designer, and photographer, and an award-winning poet, songwriter, and screenwriter, he has a twenty-five year background in the various fields of the American Civil War, thealogy (female-based religion), anthropology, etymology, and comparative mythology and religion.

The grandson of an Appalachian coal-mining family, Lochlainn is a seventh generation Kentuckian, a professional genealogist, co-chair of the Jent/Gent Family Committee (Kentucky), founder and director of the Blakeney Family Tree Project, and a board member of the Friends of Colonel Benjamin E. Caudill. Lochlainn's literary works have been endorsed by leading authorities, bestselling authors, noted scientists, and celebrated academicians from around the world.

As a professional writer Lochlainn has authored some thirty adult books ranging in scope from pro-South studies, the anthropology of religion, genealogical monographs, and Goddess-worship, to ghost stories, family histories, a comparative analysis of the origins of Christmas, and cross-cultural studies of the family and marriage. His articles, essays, interviews, and award-winning poems have been published in numerous periodicals, both nationally and internationally.

Lochlainn's eight children's books include a dictionary of religion and myth, a rewriting of the King Arthur legend (which reinstates the original pre-Christian motifs), bedtime stories for preschoolers, a naturalist's guidebook to owls, a worldwide look at the family, a scientific investigation of UFOs and aliens, and an examination of the Near-Death Experience.

Of blue-blooded Southern stock through his Kentucky, Tennessee, Virginia, West Virginia, and North Carolina ancestors, Lochlainn is a direct descendant of European royalty via his 6th great-grandfather, the Earl of Oxford, after which London's famous Harley Street was named. Among his celebrated male Celtic ancestors is Robert the Bruce, King of Scotland, Lochlainn's 22nd great-grandfather. The 21st great-grandson of Edward I "Longshanks" Plantagenet (1239-1307), King of England, Lochlainn is also a thirteenth-generation descendant of the colonists of Jamestown, Virginia (1607).

Descending from a long line of powerful women and Goddess-worshipers, some of Lochlainn's more notable female ancestors include: Queen Boudicca of the ancient Icenians (Lochlainn's 40th great-grandmother), Queen Sibyl Fitzseward of Scotland (his 27th great-grandmother), Queen Dubhehoblaigh of Ireland (34th great-grandmother), Afandreg Verch Gwair Princess of Wales (30th great-grandmother), Saint Margaret Atheling Queen of Scotland and England (26th great-grandmother), "Lady Godiva" Countess of Mercia (31st great-grandmother), Queen Matilda Baldwin of England (26th great-grandmother and the wife of William I the Conqueror), Queen Isabella "the Fair" of England (23rd great-grandmother and the wife of Edward II King of England), Queen Thyra Danebod of Denmark (32nd great-grandmother), and Empress Octavia Major Tiberius of Rome (43rd great-grandmother and the wife of Mark Anthony Emperor of Rome).

Lochlainn is a cousin of numerous notable Confederates, among them: Robert E. Lee, Nathan Bedford Forrest, Stonewall Jackson, John S. Mosby, James Longstreet, John Hunt Morgan, Jeb Stuart, States Rights Gist, George W. Gordon, Arthur M. Manigault, John Bell Hood, P. G. T. Beauregard, John H. Winder, Gideon J. Pillow, Stephen D. Lee, John C. Breckinridge, Leonidas Polk, William Giles Harding (of Belle Meade Plantation, Nashville, TN), Zebulon Vance, George Wythe Randolph (Thomas Jefferson's grandson), Felix K. Zollicoffer, Fitzhugh Lee, Benjamin E. Caudill, Nathaniel F. Cheairs (of Rippavilla Plantation, Spring Hill, TN), Jesse James, Frank James, Robert Brank Vance, Richard Taylor, Charles Sydney Winder, John W. McGavock (of Carnton Plantation, Franklin, TN), Carrie (Winder) McGavock (of Ducros Plantation, Houma, LA), David Harding McGavock (of Two Rivers Plantation, Nashville, TN), Lysander McGavock (of Midway Plantation, Brentwood, TN), James Randal McGavock (of Riverside Plantation, Franklin, TN), Randal William McGavock (of the Deery Family Home, Allisona, TN), William Henry F. Lee, Lucius E. Polk, Louisa Minor Meriwether (wife of William Andrew Charles), Sarah Knox Taylor (first wife of President Jefferson Davis), Ellen Bourne Tynes (the wife of Forrest's Chief of Artillery, Captain John W. Morton), and famed South Carolina diarist Mary Chesnut.

Lochlainn's modern day cousins include: Rebecca Gayheart (Kentucky-born actress), Shelby Lee Adams (Letcher County, Kentucky, portrait photographer), Bertram Thomas Combs (Kentucky's fiftieth governor), Edith Bolling (wife of President Woodrow Wilson), and actors Robert Duvall and Tom Cruise.

Born with music in his blood, Lochlainn is an accomplished songwriter and musician who has written some 3,000 compositions. His cousins in the music business include: Johnny Cash, Elvis Presley, Billy Ray and Miley Cyrus, Patty Loveless, Dolly Parton, Pat Boone, Lee Ann Womack, Naomi, Wynonna, and Ashley Judd, Ricky Skaggs, the Sunshine Sisters, Martha Carson, and Chet Atkins.

Lochlainn lives with his wife in historic Middle Tennessee, the heart of the Confederacy, where his conservative Southern ancestors fought and died defending Jeffersonianism, constitutional government, and personal liberty, against liberal Abraham Lincoln and the progressive North.

LOCHLAINNSEABROOK.COM

Tha gradh ag a'bhandia ort

CPSIA information can be obtained at www.ICGtesting.com
Printed in the USA
BVOW05s1713280115

385394BV00001B/53/P